German Pen Pals Made Easy

A Fun Way to Write German and Make a New Friend

Sinéad Leleu and Michaela Greck-Ismair

Brilliant
PUBLICATIONS

We hope you and your pupils enjoy corresponding with your German pen pals using this book. Brilliant Publications publishes many other books for teaching modern foreign languages. To find out more details on any of the titles listed below, please log onto our website: www.brilliantpublications.co.uk.

Published by Brilliant Publications
Unit 10
Sparrow Hall Farm
Edlesborough
Dunstable
Bedfordshire
LU6 2ES, UK

Website: www.brilliantpublications.co.uk

General information enquiries:
Tel: 01525 222292

The name Brilliant Publications and the logo are registered trademarks.

Written by Sinéad Leleu
Illustrated by James Walmesley

© Text Sinéad Leleu and Michaela Greck-Ismair 2008
© design Brilliant Publications 2008

Printed ISBN: 978-0-85747-144-4
ebook ISBN: 978-0-85747-145-1

First printed and published in the UK in 2010.
10 9 8 7 6 5 4 3 2 1

The right of Sinéad Leleu and Michaela Greck-Ismair to be identified as the authors of this work has been asserted by themselves in accordance with the Copyright, Designs and Patents Act 1988.

Contents

Introduction

In this era of technology, we MFL teachers are spoilt with an excellent array of resource material. Interactive CD-Roms, DVDs, Internet sites … you name it, we use them all. The main aim of all this is that, one day, our pupils will be able to communicate with other MFL speakers through our chosen language. In my own classes, this 'one day' is now. This, we do, through pen–pal correspondence.

My experience has shown me that, despite regularly introducing a variety of resources into my classes, rarely a class begins without a pupil asking 'Have our letters arrived yet?' 'Noch nicht' is met with disappointment whereas 'Ja' is met with great excitement and delight. My pupils are unwaveringly eager to reply. This may seem like a daunting task to the less-confident or the time-strapped teacher but …

For the teacher, *German Pen Pals Made Easy*:
- ◆ Does not require fluency
- ◆ Is time-saving – little or no preparation is required
- ◆ Links with the KS3 Programme of Study
- ◆ Has inherent cross-curricular links to geography, art and ICT
- ◆ Supplements, consolidates and revises course work

For the pupil, *German Pen Pals Made Easy*:
- ◆ Is easy to follow. The method used is gap-filling as opposed to giving pupils the daunting task of beginning with a blank page
- ◆ Is realistic. The pupil realizes that German can be used for real-life communication and not just in an artificial situation
- ◆ Instils confidence. They can communicate effectively at a basic level
- ◆ Helps foster positive attitudes towards foreign language learning
- ◆ Facilitates intercultural understanding. The pupil can learn about German culture through a German peer
- ◆ … and of course, it is fun and a wonderful way to make a new friend. (I should know as I have had the same two pen pals for over 25 years!)

Tips for the teacher

Where to find pen pals

1. There are many websites to help you to find a German-speaking class to correspond with, for example:
   - www.epals.com
   - www.globalgateway.org
   - www.etwinning.net
   - www.ipf.net.au (small fee)

   If you have the option of choosing a country, do not forget other countries where you can find German-speaking schools such as Austria and Switzerland.

2. If your town is twinned with a German town, you could contact their 'Grundschule (ages 6–9 approx), 'Hauptschule' (ages 10–14 approx), 'Realschule' (ages 10–15 approx), or 'Gymnasium' (ages 10–18 approx).

Checklist for you and your German-speaking counterpart

1. Confirm with your German-speaking counterpart that your pupils will write in German and decide whether the replies will be in English or German.

2. Decide which class will write first.

3. Decide how you are going to pair the pupils. Either one of the teachers decides or the pupils in the class that receives the first letters decide. It is a good idea to make a note of the pairs immediately as some pupils will not remember their pen pal's name. Unless you find a class with the exact same number of pupils, some pupils will have to write two letters.

4. Discuss the expected frequency of your letters. This depends on the school calendar, workload and enthusiasm. Be careful to decide on realistic deadlines. It is a good idea to take one term at a time.

5. Agree on the themes for the term ahead. Take into consideration seasonal events such as Christmas, Hallowe'en and local festivals.

Before pupils begin

1. Before pupils begin to write a letter, it is paramount to have covered the relevant language orally. Remember: **hear it, say it, see it, write it**.

2. Introduce letter writing with a sample letter written on the board, chart or overhead projector. You could use the letter for Unit 1, 'Ich stelle mich vor', on page 10; this letter can also be downloaded from our website so you can display it on a whiteboard: www.brilliantpublications.co.uk/pdfs/1043.pdf.

Highlight the five main parts of the letter:
- ◆ the heading, which includes the town and date
- ◆ the greeting
- ◆ the body of the letter
- ◆ the closing greeting
- ◆ the signature

3. Before pupils begin their first letter, explain to them how to use *German Pen Pals Made Easy*:
   - ◆ Point out that pupils must first fill in the blanks and circle where there is a choice.
   - ◆ Using imaginary details or those of a pupil in the class, go through the letter line-by-line. Complete and circle where necessary. See what pupils can come up with themselves before referring to the 'Zusätzliche Vokabeln' section.
   - ◆ Write out the entire letter on the board. Explain to pupils that they will need to write a draft into their German workbooks.
   - ◆ Tell pupils that you will then correct their draft letters before they write their final letters.

Writing your first letter

1. Having explained how to use *German Pen Pals Made Easy*, give each pupil the German template letter for 'Ich stelle mich vor' (page 10). Depending on the class level and time, some teachers will prefer to only give certain sections of the unit. For example, if your class has a good level of German, you may prefer not to hand out the English template. However, if unfinished letters are given as homework, it is advisable to give all four pages of the unit. As the templates and vocabulary are bilingual, parents/guardians will feel comfortable helping.

2. If you give the English template, point out to your pupils that they are not word-for-word translations. It is the ideas that are translated.

3. Once you have corrected the pupils' drafts, they should write their letters out neatly to send to their pen pals. Using personalized stationery can help to make their letters special. Allow the pupils to choose this for themselves.

4. If pupils wish to include attachments such as postcards, photos, drawings etc, make sure that they are either stapled or stuck to the letter or that each pupil has their own individual envelope.

As you move on

1. As soon as you receive your first replies, get your pupils to stick their letters into their German workbooks or put them into their German folders.

2. *German Pen Pals Made Easy* is flexible so, with the exception of the first unit (Ich stelle mich vor), the units may be used in any order.

3. At the beginning of the correspondence, it will be easier for pupils to stick to the template letter. However, as many pupils become more competent, encourage them to change the order of the body of the letter. Weaker pupils can continue to stick to the template letter whereas stronger pupils can use the template letter as a 'springboard'.

4. You can give the class as a whole a choice of topics to choose from. Alternate the choice between the two corresponding classes.

5. To vary the correspondence, you could use other means such as recorded messages on CD, tape, DVD or video.

6. Do not allow pupils to give their home address or telephone number (or email if you are using snail-mail) until the correspondence is well-established.

Class projects

Class projects are an excellent way to vary class correspondence. The units 'Meine Schule', 'Wo ich lebe' and 'Weihnachtszeit' are particularly suitable. The projects can be done in English with an English–German glossary. The class can be divided into small groups and given one section each. Include drawings, photos, posters, videos, DVDs, CDs, brochures etc. A class project can be sent along with individual letters or in the place of individual letters. If you have any festivals particular to where you live, this would also be interesting for your pen pals.

Here are some ideas for things that could be included in the class projects:

Meine Schule
- our class timetable
- after-school activities
- school dinners
- our uniform
- our school building
- our teachers
- our school crest
- history of our school

Wo ich lebe
- history
- a map
- landmark(s)
- festivals and celebrations
- clubs/activities for children
- food specialities
- local heroes and/or famous people
- traditional music
- languages and dialect

Weihnachtszeit
- Christmas food
- Christmas tree and decorations
- Christmas crackers
- A typical Christmas carol
- Christmas card-giving tradition
- Christmas stockings and gift-offering tradition
- 12 Days of Christmas
- Pantomimes

Classroom ideas

1. As soon as you receive your first replies, set up a 'pen pal corner' in your classroom. You can include a map of Europe, the world or the country of your pen pals, indicating where they live. You can also make flags of their country and your country. As the correspondence moves along, you can include anything that you or the pupils find interesting, such as traditional dishes, school brochures and festivals.

2. To work on oracy skills, pupils can give an oral presentation on their pen pal.

3. As part of art or ICT, pupils can make information sheets based on their pen pals with headings such as:
   - Name
   - Alter
   - Wohnort
   - Geburtstag
   - Augenfarbe
   - Haarfarbe
   - Brüder und Schwestern
   - Haustier/Lieblingstier
   - Hobby
   - Lieblingsfarbe
   - Lieblingsmusik
   - Lieblingsessen
   - Lieblingsgetränk
   - Lieblingsfach
   - Lieblingsjahreszeit

Tips for the pupil

1. Using a model letter, fill in the blanks and circle the words you would like to use. Check out the **'Zusätzliche Vokabeln'** (Extra vocabulary) section for extra vocabulary. You can keep the English translation nearby to help you.

2. Write out a draft letter (a practice letter). Your teacher will then correct it.

3. Rewrite a final copy of your letter.

4. To make your letter more interesting, use nice stationery and / or decorate your letter with colourful designs and drawings. You can use some of the ideas in the **'Zusätzliche Ideen!'** (Extra ideas!) section.

5. Enclose anything you think may interest your pen pal such as stickers, magazine cuttings, and postcards. Again, you will find ideas in the **'Zusätzliche Ideen!'** (Extra ideas!) section.

6. **Do not** give your home address, telephone number or home email address without the permission of your parents and teacher.

7. Have fun!

_____, den _____
(Ort)   (Datum)

Hallo!

Ich heisse _____ .

Ich bin_____ Jahre alt. Wie alt bist Du?

Ich lebe in _____ , in _____ .
                                          (Dein Land)
Wo lebst Du?

Ich bin ein Mädchen/Ich bin ein Junge.

Ich mag _____ und _____ .

Ich mag _____ nicht.

Bis bald!

_____
(Dein Vorname)

German Pen Pals Made Easy

_____
(town/village)

_____
(date)

Hello!

My name is _____ .

I'm _____ years old. How old are you?

I live in _____ , in _____ .
(your country)
Where do you live?

I'm a girl./I'm a boy.

I like _____ and _____ .

I don't like _____ .

Bye for now!

_____
(your first name)

Zusätzliche Vokabeln
Extra vocabulary

der Fußball	football
der Sport	sports
das Tanzen	dancing
das Basketball	basketball
das Reiten	horse riding
das Schwimmen	swimming
die Leichtathletik	athletics

die Rockmusik	rock music
die Klassische Musik	classical music
die Schule	school
das Kino	the cinema
die Horrorfilme	horror movies
die Mode	fashion
das Theater	drama / theatre
Die Simpsons	The Simpsons

die Schokolade	chocolate
die Bonbons	sweets
die Cola	cola
der Brokkoli	broccoli
die Pizza	pizza
der Spinat	spinach
der Rosenkohl	Brussels sprouts
die Eiscreme	ice-cream

(in) Frankreich	(in) France
(in) England	(in) England
(in) Schottland	(in) Scotland
(in) Wales	(in) Wales
(in) Irland	(in) Ireland

Zusätzliche Einzelheiten
Extra points

1. Boy or girl?
Your pen pal may not know from your first name if you are a girl or a boy. So, it's a good idea to tell them.

2. Ich bin zehn Jahre alt
In German we say, as in English: I am ten years old - 'ich bin zehn Jahre alt'.

3. Ich mag / Ich mag ... nicht

In English we say:	**but in German we say:**
I like football.	Ich mag Fußball.
I don't like basketball	Ich mag Basketball nicht.

'Nicht' comes after the thing you don't like.

4. Der, Die, Das, Die

der
die
das
die
} the

German Pen Pals Made Easy

der means 'the' before a masculine word, such as:	der Käse	the cheese	
	der Brokkoli	the broccoli	
	der Orangensaft	the orange juice	
die means 'the' before a feminine word, such as:	die Musik	the music	
	die Eiscreme	the ice-cream	
	die Schule	the school	
das means 'the' before a 'neutral' word, such as:	das Reiten	the horse riding	
	das Kartoffelpüree	the mashed potatoes	
	das Schwimmen	the swimming	
die means 'the' before a plural word, such as:	die Bonbons	the sweets	
	die Karotten	the carrots	
	die Horrorfilme	the horror movies	

Zusätzliche Ideen!
Extra ideas!

Include a map of your country showing where you live. Write *'Ich lebe hier'* (I live here) and draw an arrow pointing to where you live.

Ich lebe hier!

Draw or include pictures of anything that you think is particular to your country such as a double-decker bus or a red postbox.

Draw the flag of both your country and your pen pal's country on your letter page. Alternatively, you could draw a page-size flag of your country or your pen pal's country and write your letter on the flag!

Use the colour-by-number flags below to help you.

The United Kingdom Flag

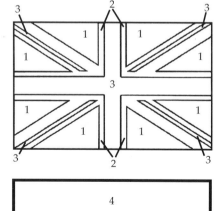

Die Deutsche Flagge

4
3
5

1 = blau
2 = weiß
3 = rot
4 = schwarz
5 = gold

_____, den _____
(Ort)   (Datum)

Lieber/Liebe _____

Vielen Dank für Deinen Brief.

Wie geht es Dir? Mir geht es _____ .

Ich habe _____ Augen und

_____ Haare.

Ich bin _____ und _____ .
(Adjektiv)   (Adjektiv)

Ich habe am _____ _____
(Tag)   (Monat)
Geburtstag.
Wann hast Du Geburtstag?

Meine Lieblingsfarbe ist _____ . Und Deine?
Welche ist Deine Lieblingsfarbe?

Schreib mir bald!
Tschüss!

_____
(Dein Vorname)

_____
(town/village)

_____
(date)

Dear _____ ,

Thank you for your letter.

How are you? I'm _____ .

I have _____ eyes and _____ hair.

I'm _____ and _____ .
        (adjective)   (adjective)

My birthday is the _____ of _____.
                    (day)   (month)
When is your birthday?

My favourite colour is _____. How about you?
What's your favourite colour?

Write soon!
Bye!

_____
(your first name)

Zusätzliche Vokabeln
Extra vocabulary

Gut	well/fine
Sehr gut	very well
Nicht gut	not well
Hallo/Tschüss	hi there/bye

hell	light
dunkel	dark
lang	long
kurz	short
lockig	curly
gerade	straight

Blau	blue
Grau	grey
Grün	green
Gelb	yellow
Braun	brown
Orange	orange
Lila/Violett	purple
Schwarz	black
Rot	red
Weiß	white

nett	nice
lustig	funny
freundlich	friendly
sensibel	sensitive
schüchtern	shy

Januar	January
Februar	February
März	March
April	April
Mai	May
Juni	June
Juli	July
August	August
September	September
Oktober	October
November	November
Dezember	December

Ich habe …	
blaue	blue
grüne	green
braune	brown
graue	grey
nussbraune	hazel
.... Augen	

Ich habe …	
blonde	blonde
hellbraune	light brown
dunkelbraune	dark brown
rote	red
..... Haare	

Zusätzliche Einzelheiten
Extra points

1. Describing your eyes and your hair

In the sentence 'I have blue eyes' – *Ich habe blaue Augen*', the 'eyes' are accusative plural, so in German we add an 'e' to the end of the adjective.

If you say 'My eyes are brown' – 'Meine Augen sind braun', then 'eyes' are nominative, so there is no ending on the adverb.

The same is true when describing your 'hair'. In German, '*Haare*' is plural so you say 'I have red hairs' – '*Ich habe rote Haare*'.

German Pen Pals Made Easy

2. Nouns

In German all nouns start with a capital letter. The months of the year are nouns, so they start with capital letters.

3. Colours

If the colours are nouns, as in the sentence 'My favourite colour is red' – '*Meine Lieblingsfarbe ist Rot*', then you use capital letters. If you describe things and use a colour as an adjective, as in 'My hairs are red' – 'Meine Haare sind rot', then you use a lower-case letter.

Zusätzliche Ideen!

Extra ideas!

Include a photo of yourself. You can stick it onto the back of your letter and write '*Das bin ich*' (It's me!)

Das bin ich!

Make up some of your own German and English expressions about your new friendship such as:

B
est
osom
uddies

F
antastic
unky
riends

F
reche   *Cheeky*
reundliche   *Friendly*
reunde   *Friend*

M
utige   *Courageous*
agische   *Magic*
ädchen   *Girl*

_____, den _____
            (Ort)   *(Datum)*

Liebe/Lieber _____

Vielen Dank für Deinen Brief und Dein Foto.

Wie geht es Dir? Mir geht es gut/sehr gut/nicht gut.

Ich habe _____ Schwester(n) und_____ Bruder (Brüder).

Meine Schwester heisst _____ . Sie ist ____ Jahre alt.

Meine Bruder heisst _____ . Er ist ____ Jahre alt.

Ich bin ein Einzelkind.

Hast du Brüder und Schwestern?

Ich habe einen/eine/ein _____, das _____
                                          (Tier)

genannt wird.

Er/Sie/Es ist_____ .
                     (Adjektiv)

Hast Du ein Haustier?

Ich habe kein Haustier, aber mein Lieblingstier ist der/die/das

_____ .
    (Tier)

Schreib mir bald!

Bis bald! Tschüss!

_____
    (Dein Vorname)

_____
(town/village)

_____
(date)

Dear _____ ,

Thank you for your letter and your photo.

How are you ? I'm fine/very well/not well.

I have ___ sister(s) and ___ brother(s).

My sister's name is _____ . She is ___ years old.

My brother's name is _____ . He is ___ years old.

I'm an only child.

Do you have brothers and sisters?

I have a _____ who is called _____ .
               (animal)

He/she is _____ .
             (adjective)

Do you have a pet ?

I don't have a pet, but my favourite animal is the

_____ .
(animal)

Write soon!

Talk soon!/Bye!

_____
(your first name)

Zusätzliche Vokabeln
Extra vocabulary

Hier ist…	Here is …
Du bist…	You are …
Das bin ich	This is me / It's me

mein Vater	my father
mein Papa	my dad
meine Mutter	my mother
meine Mama	my mum
meine Stiefmutter	my step-mother
mein Stiefvater	my step-father
mein Stiefbruder	my step-brother
meine Stiefschwester	my step-sister
meine Großmutter	my grandmother
mein Großvater	my grandfather
meine Pflegeeltern	my foster parents

eine Katze	a cat
ein Hund	a dog
ein Goldfisch	a goldfish
ein Kaninchen	a rabbit
ein Hamster	a hamster
ein Vogel	a bird
eine Maus	a mouse
eine Pferd	a horse
ein Meerschweinchen	a guinea pig

süß	sweet
drollig	funny
lästig	annoying
bezaubernd	adorable
verspielt	playful

Zusätzliche Einzelheiten
Extra points

1. Types of family

There are many types of family. Whoever you live with, you can say '*Ich lebe bei meinen* _____' (I live with _____).

2. Dear …

If your pen pal is a boy, you must translate 'Dear' to '*Lieber*'. If your pen pal is a girl, you must translate 'Dear' to '*Liebe*'.

3. More than one brother and sister

For more than one brother, you can say:

Meine Brüder heissen_____und _____ .
(My brothers' names are _____ and _____ .)

The same applies for more than one sister:

Meine Schwestern heissen_____ und _____ .
(My sisters' names are _____ and _____ .)

4. More than one pet

If you have more than one pet, you can say:

Ich habe 2 Hunde, die_____und _____ heissen .
(I have 2 dogs who are called _____ and _____.)

Don't forget to make the animal plural. Here are a few examples:

Ending with -e:

Hunde	dogs	*Ich habe 3 Hunde, 4 Goldfische und 2 Pferde.*
Goldfische	goldfish	(I have 3 dogs, 4 goldfish and 2 horses.)
Pferde	horses	

Ending with -en:

Katzen	cats	*Ich habe 3 Katzen.*
		I have 3 cats

Plural is the same as the singular:

Kaninchen	rabbits	*Ich habe 2 Kaninchen, 3 Meerschweinchen*
Meerschweinchen	guinea pigs	*und 4 Hamster.*
Hamster	hamsters	(I have 2 rabbits, 3 guinea pigs and 4 hamsters.)

Special plural forms:

Vögel	birds	*Ich habe 2 Vögel und 3 Mäuse.*
Mäuse	mice	(I have 2 birds and 3 mice.)

If you would like to describe your pets, then it is easiest to describe each pet individually:

Ich habe 2 Hunde, die Max und Molly heissen. Max ist verspielt. Molly ist bezaubernd.
(I have 2 dogs called.... .)

Zusätzliche Ideen!
Extra ideas!

Include photos of your family. You could stick a photo to the back of your letter. Draw a frame around your photo. Write *'Das bin ich'* and use an arrow to point to yourself. For other members of your family, write *'Das hier ist mein Bruder'* or *'Das hier ist mein Stiefvater'* etc and use arrows to point to the person in the photo.

Das hier ist mein Vater

Das hier ist meine Mutter

Das hier ist mein Bruder

Das bin ich

_____, den _____
(Ort)   (Datum)

Hallo/Lieber/Liebe _____

Vielen Dank für Deinen Brief/Dein Foto/Deine Fotos.
Wie geht es Dir? Mir geht es gut.

Has Du Hobbies? Ich spiele _____ /
Ich mache _____ .

Ich liebe _____, weil es Spaß macht/entspannend ist/
interessant ist/dynamisch ist/ein Teamsport ist. Und Du?
Was magst du gerne?

Ich sammle _____ .
Zur Zeit lese ich '_____'.
Ich würde gerne _____ lernen.

An meiner Schule ist das beliebteste Hobby _____ .
Wie ist das bei Dir?

Schreib mir bald!
Bis bald!!/Dein Freund/Deine
Freundin,

_____
(Dein Vorname)

_____
(town/village)

_____
(date)

Hi there/Dear _____ ,

Thank you for your letter/your photo/your photos.
How are you? I'm fine.

Do you have hobbies? I play _____ /
I do _____ .

I love _____ because it's fun/relaxing/interesting/
energetic/a team sport. How about you? What do you like?

I collect _____ .
At the moment, I'm reading '_____'.
I would like to learn to _____ .

In my school, the most popular hobby is _____ .
How about you?

Write soon!
Talk soon!/Your friend,

_____
(your first name)

Zusätzliche Vokabeln
Extra vocabulary

Ich spiele Klavier	I play piano
Ich spiele Violine	I play violin
Ich spiele Flöte	I play flute
Ich spiele Gitarre	I play guitar

Ich spiele Fußball	I play football
Ich spiele Basketball	I play basketball
Ich spiele Rugby	I play rugby
Ich spiele Volleyball	I play volleyball
Ich spiele Hockey	I play hockey
Ich spiele Golf	I play golf

Ich spiele an meiner Playstation	I play on my Playstation
Ich spiele Computerspiele	I play computer games
Ich fahre Rad	I cycle
Ich mache Gymnastik	I do gymnastics
Ich mache Judo	I do judo
Ich mache Leichtathletik	I do athletics
Ich mache Karate	I do karate
Ich gehe Reiten	I go horse riding

besonders/haupsächlich	especially
und	and
spielen	to play
ich mag ____ nicht	I don´t like
Ich hasse	I hate
Ich mag gerne	I quite like

das Schwimmen	swimming
das Lesen	reading
das Tanzen	dancing
schwimmen	to swim
lesen	to read
tanzen	to dance
die Kunst	art
das Theater	theater
fernsehen	to watch TV
Musik hören	to listen to music
ins Kino gehen	to go to the cinema

die Briefmarken	stamps
die Puppen	dolls
die Aufkleber	stickers
die Münzen	coins
die Kuscheltiere	cuddly toys
die _____karten	_____ cards

Zusätzliche Einzelheiten
Extra points

1. Sports

In German, when we speak about playing sports we say 'Ich spiele Fußball', 'Ich spiele Volleyball', 'Ich mache Leichtathletik' etc we don't use an article, so it doesn't matter if the sport is a male, female or neutral word.

2. Musical instruments

In German, when we speak about playing musical instruments we say 'Ich spiele Klavier', 'Ich spiele Gitarre' etc. We don't use an article, so it does not make any difference whether the musical instrument is a male, female or neutral word.

3. Ich mag ... – I like ...

You can use the noun or the verb to say you like something:

Ich mag Schwimmen.	or	Ich schwimme gerne.
Ich mag Lesen.	or	Ich lese gerne.
Ich mag Fußball.	or	Ich spiele gerne Fußball.
Ich mag Reiten.	or	Ich reite gerne.

If you use the noun, you need a capital letter. If you use the verb, you need to use a lower-case letter.

Zusätzliche Ideen!
Extra ideas!

Include drawings, photos or magazine cuttings of anything to do with your hobbies, eg your favourite football team, your favourite singers or you practising a hobby.

If you are interested in football, you could use the caption '*Deutschland vor, noch ein Tor!*'. This means 'Germany go for another goal!'

_____, den _____
(Ort)   (Datum)

Liebe/Lieber_____

Vielen Dank für Deinen Brief./Ich habe mich sehr über Deinen Brief

gefreut. Wie geht es Dir? Mir geht es gut/sehr gut/großartig.

Meine Schule heisst _____ .

Sie ist eine gemischte Schule/reine Mädchenschule/reine

Jungenschule/ein Internat. Ich bin im _____ Schuljahr und wir

sind _____ in meiner Klasse. Mein Lehrer/Meine Lehrerin heisst
       (Anzahl)

_____ . Er/Sie ist _____ .
                                                    (Adjektiv)

Ich trage eine Schuluniform/ Ich trage keine Schuluniform. Und Du?

Ich habe _____ Fächer: _____
          (Anzahl)   (Deine Fächer)
Mein Lieblingsfach ist_____, weil es

_____ ist.

Ich mag kein/keine _____, weil es

_____ist.

Welches ist Dein Lieblingsfach?

Schreib mir bald!

Auf Wiedersehen/Tschüss!

_____
          (Dein Vorname)

_____
(town/village)

_____
(date)

Dear _____ ,

Thank you for your letter./I was very happy to get your letter.
How are you? I'm fine/very well/great.

My school is called _____ .
It's a mixed/ girls/boys/boarding school. I'm in year_____
and there are _____ in my class. My teacher's
               (number)
name is _____ . He/She is

_____ .
(adjective)

I wear a uniform./I don't wear a uniform. How about you?

I do _____ subjects: _____ .
     (number)   *(your subjects)*
My favourite subject is _____ because it's
_____ . I don't like _____
because it's _____ . What's your favourite subject?

Write soon!
Goodbye!/Bye!

_____
(your first name)

Zusätzliche Vokabeln
Extra vocabulary

Ich liebe	I love
Ich hasse	I hate
Pause	break-time
Mittagessen	lunch

Montag	Monday
Dienstag	Tuesday
Mittwoch	Wednesday
Donnerstag	Thursday
Freitag	Friday
Samstag	Saturday
Sonntag	Sunday

die Mathematik	maths
das Englisch	English
die Geschichte	history
die Erdkunde	geography
die Musik	music
der Sport	PE
die Kunst	art
die Naturwissenschaft	science
das Französisch	French
die Staatskunde	citizenship
die Infomatik	ICT

weil	because
es ist	it is / it´s
interessant	interesting
langweilig	boring
schwierig	difficult
leicht	easy
nett	nice
streng	strict
lustig	funny
und	and

Zusätzliche Einzelheiten
Extra points

1. German and British schools

In Germany there are several types of school. Find the equivalent Klasse for your year.

Grundschule – Primary School

Germany	England, Wales & NI	Approx. age
1.Klasse	Year 1	6
2.Klasse	Year 2	7
3.Klasse	Year 3	8
4.Klasse	Year 4	9

After four years at Grundschule you decide between three types of secondary school: Hauptschule, Realschule and Gymnasium.

Germany			England, Wales & NI	Age
Hauptschule	Realschule	Gymnasium		
5.Klasse	5.Klasse	5.Klasse	Year 5	10
6.Klasse	6.Klasse	6.Klasse	Year 6	11
7.Klasse	7.Klasse	7.Klasse	Year 7	12
8.Klasse	8.Klasse	8.Klasse	Year 8	13
9.Klasse	9.Klasse	9.Klasse	Year 9	14
	10.Klasse	10.Klasse	Year 10	15
		11.Klasse	Year 11	16
		12.Klasse	Year 12	17
		13.Klasse	Year 13	18

In some German states, instead of having three different types of secondary school, there are 'Gesamtschulen', which are more like British comprehensive schools.

2. Teacher

There are no different words for teachers of different school types, but if you want to make clear in which school a teacher works, you speak of him or her as a 'Grundschullehrer', 'Hauptschullehrer', 'Realschullehrer' or 'Gynasiallehrer'.

3. Adjectives

If you are describing a female noun, you must make the adjective feminine by adding an 'e'. If you describe a male noun, you add an 'er'. For neutral nouns you add an 'es'.

ein netter Lehrer	a nice teacher (male)
eine nette Lehrerin	a nice teacher (female)
ein nettes Spiel	a nice game (neutral)

For all plural forms you always add an 'e':

nette Spiele	nice games

However, following '*Er/Sie/es ist*' (He / She / It is) you don't add an ending to the adjective:

Der Lehrer / Die Lehrerin ist nett.	The teacher is nice.
Das Spiel ist nett.	The game is nice.

4. Dein/Deine

In German there are two ways to say 'your':

Dein }
Deine } your

If the noun is masculine or neutral, we use 'Dein'
If the noun is female or plural we use 'Deine'

Zusätzliche Ideen!

Extra ideas!

Include your timetable. Write each subject in a different colour. If you don't have a timetable, ask your teacher. Here is an example from a German school to help you do your own: '*Das ist mein Studenplan*' ('Here is my timetable').

Montag	Mathematik	Kunst	Pause	Kunst	Mittag	Französisch	Englisch	Erdkunde
Dienstag	Englisch	Mathematik		Naturwissenschaften		Naturwissenschaften	Erdkunde	Englisch
Mittwoch	Geschichte	Mathematik		Englisch/Informatik		Informatik	Naturwissenschaften	Sport
Donnerstag	Französisch	Sport		Musik		Staatskunde	Mathematik/Englisch	Mathematik
Freitag	Naturwissenschaften	Sport		Geschichte		Staatskunde	Mathematik	Englisch
	9.15 Uhr	9.45 Uhr/10.15 Uhr		11.20 Uhr/12.20 Uhr		14 Uhr	14.3 Uhr/15 Uhr	15.30 Uhr

_____ , den _____
(Ort)   (Datum)

Lieber/Liebe_____ ,

Vielen Dank für Deinen Brief./Ich habe mich sehr über Deinen Brief gefreut. Ich hoffe, es geht Dir gut! Mir geht es gut/nicht schlecht/großartig!

Was isst Du gerne? Ich mag _____ und _____ .

Ich mag kein/keine/keinen _____ .

Was trinkst Du gerne? Ich mag _____ und _____ .

Ich mag kein/keine/keinen _____ .

Hier in _____ ist
(Dein Land)
' _____ '
ein traditionelles Essen.

Schreib mir bald!
Dein Freund/Deine Freundin,

_____
(Dein Vorname)

German Pen Pals Made Easy

_____
(town/village)

_____
(date)

Dear _____ ,

Thank you for your letter./I was very happy to get your letter.
I hope you are well. I'm fine/not bad/great.

What do you to eat? I like _____ and
_____ .

I don't like _____ .

What do you like to drink? I like _____ and
_____ .

I don't like _____ .

Here in _____ , '_____ '
 (your country)
is a traditional dish.

Write soon!
Your friend,

_____
(your first name)

Zusätzliche Vokabeln
Extra vocabulary

der Kaffee	coffee
der Tee	tea
die Cola	cola
der Orangensaft	orange juice
die Milch	milk
die heiße Schokolade	hot chocolate

die Ananas	pineapple
die Himbeere	raspberry
die Orange	orange
die Weintrauben	grapes
der Apfel	apple
die Rosinen	raisins

die Kartoffeln	potatoes
die Karotte	carrot
die Brokkoli	broccoli
die Spinat	spinach
der Salat	salad
der Rosenkohl	Brussels sprouts

das Vanilleeis	vanilla ice-cream
das Karameleis	caramel ice-cream
das Erdbeereis	strawberry ice-cream
die Bonbons	sweets
die Vanillesoße	custard
der Kuchen	cake
die Schokolade	chocolate

das Käsebrot	cheese sandwich
das Schinkenbrot	ham sandwich
das Kartoffelpüree	mashed potatoes
das Omelette	omelette
die Suppe	soup
die Pommes frittes	chips
die Quiche	quiche
die Chips	crisps
das Hacksteak	burger

Ich liebe	I love
Ich mag gerne	I quite like
Ich hasse	I hate
lecker, lecker	Yum, yum
Igitt!	Yuck!

Zusätzliche Einzelheiten
Extra points

1. Your friend
If you are talking about a boy, you use *'Dein Freund'*. If you are talking about a girl, you use *'Deine Freundin'*. we add an 'in' to *'Freund'* to make it feminine.

2. German dishes
In some parts of Germany you can eat *'Sauere Lunge und Leber'* (this means 'sour lung and liver'): small pieces of lung and liver in a sour sauce, usually served with a dumpling). In other parts they eat *'Saumagen'* (this means 'stomach of a female pig'); it is indeed the stomach stuffed with meat and vegetables). You could ask your pen pal:

Hast Du schon mal 'Saure Lunge und Leber' oder 'Saumagen' gegessen?
(Have you ever tasted 'sour lung and liver' or 'stomach'?)

Zusätzliche Ideen!
Extra ideas!

Include the recipe for the traditional dish you have chosen. You can write this in English but look up the ingredients in a bilingual dictionary and include a mini-glossary.

Design your perfect menu. Put it on the back of your letter. Use the example below to help you.

Das ist mein ideales Menü!
(Here is the ideal menu!)

_____'s
(Dein Vorname)

Menü

*Steak mit Pommes frittes
oder
Kartoffelpuree mit
Wurstchen*

*Cola
oder
Orangensaft*

*Schokoladeneis
oder
Vanilleeis*

_____, den _____
(Ort)   (Datum)

Hallo! Lieber/Liebe_____,

Ich habe mich sehr über Deinen Brief gefruet. Vielen Dank!

Wie geht es Dir? Mir geht es gut/großartig!

Wie läuft Dein Tag ab? Ich stehe um _____ Uhr auf.

Wann stehst Du auf? Die Schule fängt um _____ Uhr an. Und

Deine Schule?

Ich esse um _____ Uhr zu Mittag und verlasse die

Schule um _____Uhr. Und Du?

Mein Abendessen ist um _____ . Uhr und ich gehe um

_____Uhr zu Bett. Wann gehst Du zu Bett?

Welche ist Deine Lieblingsjahreszeit? Meine Lieblingsjahreszeit ist

der _____, weil ich _____mag und

wenn es _____.
(Das Wetter)

Schreib mir bald!

Bis bald/Tschüss!

_____
(Dein Vorname)

_____ _____

_____
(town/village)

_____
(date)

Hi there!/Dear _____ ,

I was delighted to get your letter. Thank you very much.
How are you? I'm fine/great.

How is your day? I get up at _____ a.m. What time do you get
up? School starts at _____ a.m. What about your school?

I have lunch at _____ p.m. and I leave school at
_____ p.m. How about you?

I have dinner at _____ and I go to bed at _____ .
What time do you go to bed?

What's your favourite season? My favourite season is
_____ because I love _____
and when it _____ .
(the weather)

Write soon!
Talk soon!/Bye!

_____
(your first name)

Zusätzliche Vokabeln
Extra vocabulary

Ich frühstücke	I eat breakfast
Ich gehe aus dem Haus	I leave home
Ich erreiche die Schule	I get to school
Ich schlafe	I sleep
Ich mache/spiele nach der Schule	I do after-school activities
Ich schaue fern	I watch TV
Ich lese	I read

Frühling	spring
Sommer	summer
Herbst	autumn
Winter	winter

es ist schön	it´s fine
es ist sonnig	it´s sunny
es schneit	it´s snowing
es ist windig	it´s windy
es ist heiß	it´s hot
es regnet	it´s raining
es ist kalt	it´s cold

Weihnachten	Christmas
die Schulferien	the school holiday
Halloween	Halloween
Osterferien	Easter Holiday
mein Geburtstag	my birthday
zum Strand gehen	to go to the beach
Herbstfarben	autumn colours
die Narzissen/ die Osterglocken	the daffodils
einen Schneemann bauen	to make a snowman
eine Schneeballschlacht machen	to have a snowball fight

Zusätzliche Einzelheiten
Extra points

Time

In English, we usually use a.m. and p.m. to differentiate between morning and evening. In German, it is more common to use the 24 hour clock.

1 a.m. = 1 Uhr	7 a.m. = 7 Uhr	1 p.m. = 13 Uhr	7 p.m. = 19U hr
2 a.m. = 2 Uhr	8 a.m. = 8 Uhr	2 p.m. = 14 Uhr	8 p.m. = 20 Uhr
3 a.m. = 3 Uhr	9 a.m. = 9 Uhr	3 p.m. = 15 Uhr	9 p.m. = 21 Uhr
4 a.m. = 4 Uhr	10 a.m. = 10 Uhr	4 p.m. = 16 Uhr	10 p.m. = 22 Uhr
5 a.m. = 5 Uhr	11 a.m. = 11 Uhr	5 p.m. = 17 Uhr	11 p.m. = 23 Uhr
6 a.m. = 6 Uhr	12 p.m. = 12 Uhr	6 p.m. = 18 Uhr	12 a.m. = 24 Uhr

You would write 8.15 a.m. as 8.15 Uhr, but when you say it aloud you would say 'acht Uhr fünfzehn'.

Zusätzliche Ideen!
Extra ideas!

Fill in the times in the following daily routine.

Ich stehe um _____ Uhr auf.

Ich frühstücke um _____ Uhr.

Ich erreiche die Schule um _____ Uhr.

Ich esse um _____ Uhr zu Mittag.

Ich verlasse die Schule um _____ Uhr.

Ich spiele um _____ Uhr.

Ich esse um _____ Uhr zu abend.

Ich gehe um _____ Uhr zu Bett.

To make your daily routine more interesting, why not add speech bubbles.
You could fill them with comments such as:

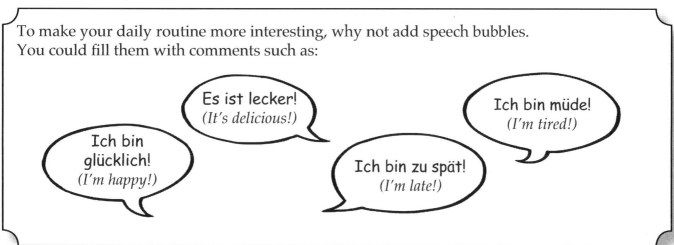

Es ist lecker!
(It's delicious!)

Ich bin müde!
(I'm tired!)

Ich bin glücklich!
(I'm happy!)

Ich bin zu spät!
(I'm late!)

_____, den _____
(Ort)   (Datum)

Hallo/Lieber/Liebe_____,

Wie geht es Dir?
Mir geht es gut, Danke/Mir geht es großartig, Danke.

Ich lebe in _____. Das ist ein Dorf/eine
Stadt/eine Großstadt/auf dem Land.
Es ist _____.
                        (Adjektiv)
Es gibt _____ Einwohner. Wie ist Deine Stadt/ Dein Dorf?

In _____ gibt es ein Schwimmbad/eine Bücherei/
      (Deine Stadt)
einen Supermarkt/ein Krankenhaus/ein Rathaus/ein Cafe/einen
Gasthof/ein Kino/eine Schule/einen Park/eine Apotheke/einen
Metzger/ eine Bäckerei/eine Burg/einen Fluss/eine Kirche.

Jedes Jahr im _____ feiern wir _____
                                              (Brauch/Sitte)
_____/haben wir einen Jahrmarkt.
Wie ist das bei Dir?

Schreib mir bald!
Auf Wiedersehen/Tschüss/Dein
Freund/Deine Freundin,

_____
(Dein Vorname)

_____
(town/village)

_____
(date)

Hello/Dear _____ ,

How are you?
I'm fine, thanks./I'm great, thanks.

I live in _____ . It's a village/a town/a city/in the
country. It's _____ . There are _____
                    (adjective)
inhabitants. What's your town/your village like?

In _____ , there is a swimming pool/a library/a
        (your town/ village)
supermarket/a hospital/a town hall/a café/a restaurant/a cinema
/a school/a park/a pharmacy/a butcher/a bakery/a castle/a river
/a church.

Every year in the month of _____, we celebrate
_____ /we have a carnival.
                (custom/tradition)
How about you?

Write soon!
Goodbye!/Bye!/Your friend,

_____
        (your first name)

Zusätzliche Vokabeln
Extra vocabulary

eine Bank	a bank
ein Stadion	a stadium
ein Laden	a shop
ein Museum	a museum
ein Postamt	a post office
ein Markt	a market
eine Eislaufbahn	an ice-rink
eine Strasse	a road
ein Bahnhof	a train station
ein Flughafen	a airport
eine Fabrik	a factory

an/am/auf	on
eine Insel	an island
am Meer	on the seaside
bei/in der Nähe von	near

geschäftig	busy
groß	big
laut	noisy
schön	pretty
friedlich	peaceful
klein	small
reizend/ hübsch	beautiful/nice
nett	nice
ruhig	calm
langweilig	boring
lebhaft	lively

ein Volksfest/ Kirmes/Dult	fair
das Chinesische Neue Jahr	the Chinese New Year
Tag des Heiligen Georgs	Saint George´s Day
Pfannkuchentag	Pancake Day
Tag des Heiligen Andreas	Saint Andrew´s Day
Maifeiertag	May Day
die Osterparade	the Easter parade

Zusätzliche Einzelheiten
Extra points

1. Prepositions to describe where you live

You can give a clearer idea of where you live by using prepositions, for example:

Es liegt bei Leeds/Manchester/London/Stonehenge.
(It's near Leeds....)

Es liegt am Meer
(It's by the seaside)

Es liegt auf einer Insel
(It's on an island)

Es liegt auf der Insel _____.
(It´s on the Isle of_)

'*Es ist*' literally means '*it is*', but if you describe places in German, it's better to say '*Es liegt*'.

2. Adjectives

You can also use adjectives to describe buildings and public places. Don't forget, the adjectives go before the noun in German. Make sure to use the correct ending:' -es' for neutral, '-e' for female and '-er' for masculine nouns. For example:

ein schönes Museum	a nice museum
ein schönes Schwimmbad	a nice swimming pool
ein grosse Bücherei	a big library
eine grosse Kirche	a big church
ein kleiner Flughafen	a small airport
ein kleiner Markt	a small market

3. Plurals

In German '*ein*' has no plural like in English. For example:

Es gibt ein Restaurant.	There is a restaurant.
Es gibt Restaurants.	There are restaurants.
Es gibt eine Bank.	There is a bank.
Es gibt Banken.	There are banks.

4. Famous for anything?

If the area where you live is famous or known for anything such as a market, a sporting event, a famous person, a particular type of food or an historical event, you can say:

_____ *ist berühmt/bekannt für* _____ .
(Deine Stadt)

(_____ is famous / known for _____ .)
(your town)

Zusätzliche Ideen!
Extra ideas!

Include tourist guides or brochures of your village/town/city or county.

Draw a plan of your town/village or an area of where you live. Label your plan in German.

eine Kirche *eine Schule*

ein Park

Hier wohne ich

Kleidung:

_____, den _____
(Ort)   (Datum)

Hi/Hallo/Lieber/Liebe_____,

Wie geht es Dir? Mir geht es gut/nicht gut.
Vielen Dank für Deinen Brief.

Magst Du Mode? Ich liebe/hasse Mode.

Am Wochenende ziehe ich gerne _____ und
_____ an. Ich mag _____
                                        (Adjektiv)
Kleidung. Und Du?

In der Schule trage ich eine Uniform. Das ist Pflicht./Ich trage
keine Schuluniform. Hast Du eine Schuluniform?

Ich trage eine _____Jacke/_____Hosen
                (Farbe)   (Farbe)
ein _____Hemd/einen _____Rock
     (Farbe)   (Farbe)
ein _____Kleid/eine _____Kravatte
     (Farbe)   (Farbe)
einen_____Trainingsanzug/_____Socken.
      (Farbe)   (Farbe)
Ist das nicht_____!
              (Adjektiv)

Schreib mir bald!
Dein Freund/Deine Freundin/Tschüss/
liebe Grüße,

_____
(Dein Vorname)

_____
(town/village)

_____
(date)

Hello / Dear _____ ,

How are you? I'm fine / not well.
Thanks a lot for your letter.

Do you like fashion? I love /hate fashion.

At the weekend, I like to wear _____ and
_____ . I like _____ clothes. How about you?
(adjective)

I wear a uniform to school. It's compulsory./I don't wear a uniform.
Do you wear a uniform?

I wear a _____ jumper/_____ trousers
            (colour)   *(colour)*
a _____ shirt/a _____ skirt
    (colour)   *(colour)*
a _____ dress/a _____ tie
    (colour)   *(colour)*
a _____ tracksuit/_____ socks.
    (colour)   *(colour)*
_____ , isn't it?
        (adjective)

Write soon!
Your friend/Bye!/Love,

_____
(your first name)

Zusätzliche Vokabeln
Extra vocabulary

gross	big
klein	small
lang	long
kurz	short
altmodisch	old-fashioned

eine Jeans	jeans
ein T-Shirt	a t-shirt
ein Sweatshirt	a sweatshirt
Turnschuhe	trainers
ein Kleid	a dress
ein Schal	a scarf
eine Mütze	a cap
eine Jacke	a jacket
ein Hut	a hat
ein Mantel	a coat
eine Bluse	a blouse
ein Trikot	a jersey

rot	red
orange	orange
gelb	yellow
grün	green
blau	blue
violett	purple
schwarz	black
braun	brown
weiß	white
grau	grey
marineblau	navy

modisch	fashionable
schick	trendy
altmodisch	old-fashioned
bequem	comfortable
einfach	simple
bunt	brightly coloured
schön	lovely
schrecklich	awful

normalerweise	usually
manchmal	sometimes

Zusätzliche Einzelheiten
Extra points

1. Adjective agreement

Colours are adjectives, so they need to agree with the noun they are describing.

If the noun is masculine, you need to use the masculine form of the colour:

ein **blauer** Pullover	a blue jumper
ein **grüner** Hut	a green hat

If the noun is feminine, you need to use the feminine form of the colour:

eine **blaue** Jacke	a blue jacket
eine **grüne** Bluse	a green blouse

If the noun is neutral, you need to use the neutral form of the colour:

ein **blaues** Hemd a blue shirt
ein **rotes** Kleid a red dress

If the noun is plural, you must add an 'e' to the colour:

blau**e** Hosen blue trousers
grün**e** Blusen green blouse
rot**e** Kleider red dresses

2. Liebe Grüße:

German children often use 'Liebe Grüße' as their closing greeting. This literally means 'lovely greetings'. The English equivalent would probably be 'love'.

Zusätzliche Ideen!

Extra ideas!

Meine Lieblingskleidung (My favourite outfit)

Draw your favourite outfit under your letter or include a photo of you wearing your favourite outfit, sports gear or uniform.

_____, den _____
(Ort)   (Datum)

Hallo/Lieber/Liebe_____,

Danke für Deinen Brief. Ich habe mich sehr über ihn gefreut. Ich hoffe, Dir geht es gut.

Ich wohne in einem/einer _____.
(Art des Hauses/der Wohnung)

Es/Sie hat _____ Zimmer.

Es gibt ein _____, ein _____,

ein_____, und ein _____.

Ich habe ein eigenes Zimmer./Ich teile mein Zimmer

mit_____. In meinem Zimmer gibt es

_____, _____ und _____.

Wir haben auch einen_____ Garten/einen Balkon mit

_____.

Schreib mir bald und beschreibe Dein Haus/
Deine Wohnung.

Tschüss/Bis bald!/Dein Freund/
Deine Freundin,

_____
(Dein Vorname)

German Pen Pals Made Easy

_____
(town/village)

_____
(date)

Hello/Dear _____ ,

Thank you for your letter. I was delighted to get it.
I hope you are well.

I live in a/an _____ . There are _____ rooms.
(type of house)
There is _____ , _____ , _____
and _____ .

I have my own bedroom./I share my bedroom with

_____ . In my bedroom, there is _____ ,

_____ and _____ .

We also have a _____ garden/balcony with

_____ .

Write soon and describe your house!

Bye!/Talk soon!/Your friend,

_____
(your first name)

Zusätzliche Vokabeln
Extra vocabulary

ein Keller	a cellar
eine Küche	a kitchen
ein Wohnzimmer	a sitting room
ein Schlafzimmer	a bedroom
ein Arbeitszimmer	an office
ein Spielezimmer	a playroom
ein Wintergarten	a conservatory
ein Badezimmer	a bathroom
ein Dachboden	an attic
eine Garage	a garage
ein Esszimmer	a dining room

meine Schwester	my sister
meine Schwestern	my sisters
mein Bruder	my brother
meine Brüder	my brothers

groß	big
klein	small
eine Blume	a flower

Schaukeln	swings
ein Baum	a tree
ein Basketballkorb	a basketball ring

ein Bett	a bed
ein Nachttisch	a bedside table
ein TV-Gerät	a TV
ein Fernseher	a television
ein Kleiderschrank	a wardrobe
ein Läufer	a rug
ein CD-Spieler	a CD player
eine Kommode	a chest of drawers
ein Poster	a poster
ein Regal	a shelf

ein Haus	a house
ein Appartement	an apartment
ein Caravan	a caravan
ein Hausboot	a houseboat

Zusätzliche Einzelheiten
Extra points

1. Plurals

If you have more than one of a certain room or piece of furniture, don't forget to make the noun plural. For example:

Es gibt einen Kleiderschrank.	There is a wardrobe.
Es gibt vier Kleiderschränke.	There are four wardrobes.

Es gibt ein Regal.	There is a shelf.
Es gibt zwei Regale.	There are two shelfs.

However, to make 'Zimmer' (room) plural, you do not make any changes to the word!

Es gibt ein Schlafzimmer	There is one bedroom.
Es gibt vier Schlafzimmer	There are four bedrooms.

2. 1 or a

The number '1' and the word 'a' are both translated into 'ein' or 'eine', so

There is 1 bedroom

There is a bedroom
} Es gibt ein Schafzimmer.

There is 1 chest of drawers

There is a chest of drawers
} Es gibt eine Kommode.

But: if you are counting 1, 2, 3….(one, two, three…) you translate '1' (one) into 'eins':
1, 2, 3… (eins, zwei, drei..)!

Zusätzliche Ideen!
Extra ideas!

Include a photo or drawing of your house or apartment block.

Mein Zimmer (my bedroom)/Mein Wunschzimmer (my ideal bedroom)
Draw a plan of your bedroom or of your ideal bedroom.

ein Fernseher

ein CD-Spieler

ein Kleiderschrank

ein Läufer

eine Kommode

ein Bett

ein Nachttisch

_____, den _____
(Ort)   (Datum)

Lieber/Liebe_____,

Danke für Deinen Brief./Ich war sehr glücklich, Deinen Brief zu bekommen. Ich hoffe, Dir geht es gut. Mir geht es gut/sehr gut/ großartig.

Ich liebe/Ich mag Weihnachten. Und Du?

In _____ feiern viele Familien Weihnachten.
(Dein Land)
Die Kinder hängen Socken an den Kamin. Santa Klaus hinterlässt Geschenke in ihnen.

Am 1.Weihnachtsfeiertag essen wir mit _____zu Mittag.
Wir haben_____. Und Du? Nach dem Essen ziehen wir an Knallbonbons.

Dieses Weihnachten wünsche ich mir_____.
(ein Geschenk)
Und Du?

Frohe Weihnachten und ein Gutes Neues Jahr!
Dein Freund/Deine Freundin,

_____
(Dein Vorname)

_____
(town/village)

_____
(date)

Dear _____ ,

Thank you for your letter./I was very happy to get your letter.

I hope you are well. I'm fine/very well/great.

I love/I like Christmas. How about you?

In _____ many families celebrate Christmas.
(your country)
The children leave stockings on the chimney. Santa Claus leaves
presents in them.

On Christmas Day, I have dinner with _____ . We
eat _____ . How about you? After dinner, we pull
'crackers'.

This Christmas, I would like _____ . How about
(a present)
you?

Merry Christmas and Happy New Year!
Your friend,

_____
(your first name)

Zusätzliche Vokabeln
Extra vocabulary

Heiligabend	Christmas Eve
die Krippe	the crib
eine Weihnachtstorte	a Christmas log
ein Christbaum	a Christmas tree
die Dekoration	decorations
das Lametta	tinsel
ein Stern	a star

in England	in England
in Irland	in Ireland
in Schottland	in Scotland
in Wales	in Wales

ein Skateboard	a skateboard
ein Videospiel	a video game
ein Computer	a computer
eine CD	a CD
ein Mobiltelefon	a mobile phone
ein Fahrrad	a bike
Inline-Skates	roller blades
ein Buch	a book
eine DVD	a DVD

Truthahn	turkey
gebackene Kartoffel	roast potatoes
Karrotten	carrots
Rosenkohl	Brussels sprouts
ein 'Mince Pie' (eine mit gehackten Früchten gefüllte Teigtasche)	a mince pie
ein 'Christmas' Pudding' (ein schwerer Früchtekuchen)	a Christmas pudding

Zu Mittag esse ich mit…	
meiner Mutter	my mother
meinem Vater	my father
meiner Schwester	my sister
meinem Bruder	my brother
meinen Großeltern	my grandparents
meinem Cousin	my cousin (male)
meiner Cousine	my cousin (female)

Zusätzliche Einzelheiten
Extra points

1. Christmas cards
In Germany, people do send Christmas cards, but only to close friends and to their family.

2. Stockings for Santa?
In Germany, children don´t leave out stockings at Christmas. On Christmas Eve, when it becomes dark outside, a Christmas bell rings and the children are allowed to enter a room that up until this time has been locked. There they find their presents under the decorated Christmas tree. The family sings some Christmas Carols and then the children are allowed to open their presents.

3. Crackers

Pulling crackers is not a German tradition.

Zusätzliche Ideen!
Extra ideas!

Although sending Christmas cards isn't as popular in Germany as it is in the United Kingdom, you could make a card to send to your pen pal. Write a greeting such as:

Frohe Weihnachten und ein Gutes Neues Jahr
(Merry Christmas and Happy New Year)

As most German people don't usually know about Christmas crackers, you could make one for your pen pal. You will need:

◆ a toilet paper roll
◆ crêpe paper
◆ a ribbon
◆ goodies such as sweets, a paper hat, a small toy

Don't put a snapper in as it is illegal to post them overseas.

Instructions
◆ Fill the roll with some goodies.
◆ Wrap the roll in the crêpe paper.
◆ Gather the crêpe paper at both ends of the roll and tie with the ribbon.
◆ As your pen pal may not know what to do with the cracker, include the following instructions:

> *Zwei Personen halten je ein Ende und ziehen. Die Person mit dem größeren Teil darf den Inhalt behalten.*
>
> (Two people hold an end each and pull. The person with the biggest piece gets to keep the contents.)

_____, den _____
(Ort)   (Datum)

Lieber/Liebe_____/Hi!

Vielen Dank für Deinen Brief. Ich fand Deinen Brief sehr schön.
Danke!

Bald sind Sommerferien. _____!

Wenn ich an die Ferien denke, denke ich an_____,

_____ und_____. Und Du? Woran

denkst Du?

Im _____ fahre/fliege ich nach
        (Monat)

_____ mit _____/
        (ein Land/eine Stadt)

werde ich mich zu Hause erholen. Und Du? Gehst du in die Ferien?

Ich werde auch _____. Was machst Du
                    (eine Freizeitbeschäftigung machen)

diesen Sommer?

Heute ist es_____/Heute _____ es.
            (Adjektiv)   (Verb)
Wie ist das Wetter bei Dir?

Schreib mir bald!
Bis bald! Dein Freund/Deine Freundin,

_____
(Dein Vorname)

_____
(town/village)

_____
(date)

Dear _____ /Hi!

Thank you for your letter./I loved your letter. Thank you!

The summer holidays are coming. _____ !

When I think of the holidays, I think of _____ ,
_____ and _____ . How about
you? What do you think of?

In _____ , I'm going
        (month)
_____ with
        (to a country/ a town)
_____ /I'm going to relax at home.
How about you? Are you going on holidays?

I'm also going to _____ . What are you
                        (do an activity)
going to do this summer?

Today, it's _____ . What's the weather like over there?

Write soon!
Talk soon!/Your friend,

_____
(your first name)

Zusätzliche Vokabeln
Extra vocabulary

Großartig	great
Fantastisch	fantastic
Herrlich	wonderful
Hurra	yippee

in ein Sommer-lager gehen	to go to a summer camp
in ein Ferienlager gehen	to go to a holiday camp

der Strand	beach
die Sonne	sun
Ausschlafen	lie-in
Sandburg	sand castle
das Meer / die See	the sea
das Picknick	picnic
Eiscreme	ice-cream

Fußball spielen	to play football
Basketball spielen	to play basketball
einen Deutschkurs machen	to do German classes
Reiten gehen	to go horse riding
spielen	to play games
Zelten gehen	to go camping

meine Familie	my family
meine Eltern	my parents
meine Großeltern	my grandparents
meine Cousins / meine Cousinen	my cousins

es ist schön	it's fine
es ist sonnig	it's sunny
es regnet	it's raining
es ist heiß	it's hot
es ist kalt	it's cold
es ist windig	it's windy

Zusätzliche Einzelheiten
Extra points

1. Ich denke an : den, die, das...

If you want to say 'I think of…' you say '*Ich denke an…*'. We know that der, die, and das all mean 'the'. This changes with masculine nouns, not with female and neutral nouns. For example:

Ich denke an den Strand. (masculine)   I think of the beach.
Ich denke an die Sonne. (feminine)   I think of the sun.
Ich denke an das Meer. (neutral)   I think of the sea.

For masculine nouns, you need to change the translation of "the" from "der Strand" to "den Strand" because it is not the nominative case.

The same is true for:

Ich gehe an den Strand.
(I'm going to the beach.)

Ich gehe au das Meer.
(I'm going to the sea.)

But:

Der Strand ist schön.
(The beach is wide.)

2. Ich fahre nach/Ich fliege nach (I am going to)...

If you are going to another town or country you say usually *'Ich fahre nach'* ('I drive to') if you go by car, bus or train, or *'Ich fliege nach'* ('I fly to') if you go by airplane.

If you translate 'going' to *'gehen'*, this would mean you really walk to another place.

Ich fahre nach Blackpool.
(I´m going to Blackpool.)

Ich fliege nach Deutschland.
(I´m going to Germany.)

Ich gehe zum Laden.
(I´m going to the shop.)

Zusätzliche Ideen!
Extra ideas!

Include a map of Europe. Use arrows to point to countries you would like to visit:

Das sind die Länder, die ich gerne besuchen würde.
(Here are the countries I would like to visit.)

If you have visited some of these countries, you can say:

Das sind die Länder, die ich besucht habe.
(Here are the countries I have visited.)

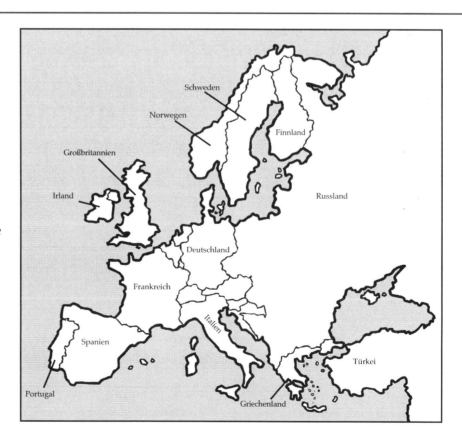

Lightning Source UK Ltd.
Milton Keynes UK
03 November 2010

162335UK00008B/1/P